THE *ZIP ZAP KID*
AND THE
HANDBAG

Written by Alison Hawes
Illustrated by Andy Rowland

I am Jez.
But in seconds, I am
the Zip Zap Kid!

A man has Mum's handbag.
Mum wants it back!

In seconds, I am
the Zip Zap Kid!

Mum has some mints in her bag.
I toss the tin of mints at the man.

The man lets go of Mum's handbag.
He limps off.

Mum picks up her handbag.
She has it back at last.

But she can't have her tin of
mints back.
It is bent and dented!